PROFITABLE WONDERS

PROFITABLE WONDERS

ASPECTS OF THOMAS TRAHERNE

A. M. Allchin Anne Ridler
Julia Smith

THE AMATE PRESS

ISBN 0 947561 17 X

Printed in Great Britain
by Parchment (Oxford) Ltd

Contents

Preface

Thomas Traherne is a writer who is at once well known and yet unknown. The famous passages of poetic prose which have found their way into so many anthologies have given many readers a first glimpse of his vision. But to be fully appreciated they need to be seen in the context of his work as a whole. This has not always happened in the past, and indeed it cannot happen fully until more of his unpublished work has been published. The story of the gradual rediscovery of Traherne's manuscripts during this century is full of unlikely happenings. It inevitably suggests the thought that Traherne may be among those writers like Julian of Norwich who have written more for subsequent ages than for their own.

In this book we have approached Traherne in three different but complementary ways. Anne Ridler, herself a poet and an editor of Traherne, presents the heart of his vision of the glory of God revealed in his creation, and considers him as a master of the affirmative way. Julia Smith introduces us to some of the fascinating material to be found in the as yet unpublished writings of Traherne, and in doing so shows us new dimensions of this remarkable man. We gain a new understanding of the extent of his interests and of his place in the life of his own post-restoration period. In my own essay, which draws largely on the unpublished manuscript in the Bodleian, called *The Church's Year Book*, I have tried to show Traherne as a true and balanced representative of the Anglican teaching of his time, with its sacramental vision of the world, its delight in the communion of saints, and its longing for greater unity, and in doing so have, I hope, shown something of his affinity with the theology of the first Christian millennium, which in its Eastern form gave particular importance to the contemplation of nature, *theoria physike*.

Since its beginnings in the autumn of 1987 the St Theosevia Centre for Christian Spirituality has organised a number of study days at its centre in Canterbury Road, Oxford. The subjects of these days have ranged widely, from 'The Spirituality of

Icons' to 'The Experience of Depression'; from 'St Isaac of Syria' to 'The Hymns of Charles Wesley'.

Traherne formed the subject of our meeting on 25 February 1989, and the three lectures given then make up the substance of this book. It is the aim of the Centre both to study and promote the Christian spiritual tradition. The writings of Traherne proved themselves unexpectedly appropriate for our attention. Rooted in their own time they have surprising relevance for today.

A spiritual writer for whom the creation plays so central a role in the relationship between man and God, who is not afraid to praise God for the body as well as for the soul, has much to say to a time like ours, which is searching for a new and better appreciation of our responsibility for the material environment. In his sense of our co-inherence with one another and with the whole creation, Traherne speaks powerfully to a society which needs to correct the imbalances brought about by a divisive individualism.

A. M. Allchin

Easter 1989

The Essential Traherne

ANNE RIDLER

Thomas Traherne, known to us through his writings, is a great master of the Affirmative Way – the pursuit of perfection through the knowledge and love of God's created world. Felicity is Traherne's word for the goal sought on this Way, and although his method of exposition, and the principles he followed, have an ancestry in earlier Christian writings, he is truly original, and independent of much of the thought of his time, in his emphasis on the natural goodness of man – man as stamped with the image of his creator. Louis Martz, in his seminal book *The Paradise Within*, puts it thus:

> Traherne here displays his greatest originality and independence of mind, shaking off those bitter conceptions of man's depravity that played so large a part in contemporary thought: the doctrine that Augustine developed in his anti-Pelagian writings, and which descended from him to find its place in the ninth of the Thirty-Nine Articles of the English Church. (Original Sin is the 'fault and corruption of the Nature of every man'.)[1]

If we knew no other work of Traherne besides his *Centuries of Meditations*, we should still possess his essential thought – the cream of his work, to use a favourite seventeenth-century expression – and in this essay I propose to concentrate on the *Centuries*, with only passing references elsewhere. The other essays in this book cover different aspects of his work, both published and unpublished.

What we know of Traherne's history makes but a short chapter, if we exclude the attempts that have been made to fill out the story by guesswork. He was born in 1637 of a Herefordshire shoemaker, who died when Thomas and his younger brother Philip were small. Thomas writes in the *Centuries* of his father's 'poor house' where he enjoyed 'few and obscure comforts'; but we know from one of Aubrey's *Reminiscences*, said to be derived from Traherne himself, that his father employed two apprentices, and Thomas received an education which fitted him for a university. Aged fifteen or sixteen (the usual age in those days), he enrolled at Brasenose College, Oxford, where he followed the prescribed course of studies for a degree – philosophy, ancient languages, mathematics. This satisfied him very well except that, as he later wrote, 'There was never a Teacher that did professely Teach Felicity, though that be the mistress of all other Sciences.' He took his BA in 1656, and in the following year, still under the Commonwealth (and therefore still nominally a Puritan) he was appointed to the cure of Credenhill, a small parish about five miles from Hereford. After the Restoration of 1660, he received Anglican ordination and was again appointed to the parish with different sponsors. In this same year of 1661, according to the Brasenose register, he was created MA. A contemporary account by George Hickes, the Non-juror, refers to the procedure required for this degree. The candidate, with his lambswool hood thrown back, had to walk from college to college, offering himself for examination, and Hickes overheard a Frenchman conjecture that he must be doing penance for some great crime.

At Credenhill Traherne lived the life of a faithful pastor, taking it as his vocation (to quote one of his notebooks):

> to teach Immortal Souls the way to Heaven, to sanctifie God's Sabbaths, to instruct them in His Laws given upon Mount Sinai, and to show them the Love of a Glorious Saviour slain upon mount Calvary: to Lead them by His Merits to Eternal Joys.[2]

It seems that Traherne must have continued at Credenhill for at least the next eight years, but at some point he took time to work in Oxford at a dissertation on Roman Catholic Forgeries. In the Preface to this book Traherne gives a brief picture of himself as descending one evening from his work in the Bodleian Library – 'which is the Glory of Oxford, and this Nation' – and being required to speak with 'a Grave Person, in the Quadrangle, a man that had spent many thousand pounds in promoting Popery', whom forthwith he took to walk 'in the New-Parks' for greater liberty and privacy for their discussion. But it was profitless, for Traherne found him 'obdurate' and impervious to reason.

Roman Forgeries was the only work that Traherne published in his lifetime: it appeared in 1673, a year before his death, and had probably been offered for his Bachelorhood of Divinity, which he received in 1669. But to judge from the amount of work which has so far (and so strangely) come to light, there can have been few days in his short life when his pen was not at work. From the natural flow of his prose, one would guess that writing came to him as easily as speaking; and that he was a voluble, even exuberant, talker we know from two sources: one, an anonymous Preface to his posthumously published 'Thanksgivings' (I give its short title – it appeared in 1699), and the other, Traherne himself. This last is an engaging piece of self-criticism written in one of his notebooks:

Profound Inspection, Reservation and Silence are my Desires. O that I could attain them: Too much openness and proneness to speak are my Diseas...Speaking too much and too Long in the Best Things...Here I am Censured for speaking in the singular number and saying I...'

[then ruefully] 'Felicitie is a Bird of Paradice so strang, that it is Impossible to flie among men without Loseing some feathers were she not Immortall.'[3]

The account of him in the anonymous Preface says that on this subject of Felicity and the love of God towards mankind he dwelt continually when at home, and when he went out 'was so full of them that those who would converse with him were forced to endure some discourse upon these subjects, whether they had any sense of Religion, or not. And therefore to such he might sometimes be thought troublesome, but his company was very acceptable to all such as had any inclinations to Virtue, and Religion.' As to his character in general, the same source tells us, he was 'of a cheerful and sprightly temper, free from any thing of the sourness and formality, by which some great pretenders of Piety rather disparage and misrepresent true Religion, than recommend it; and therefore was very affable and pleasant in his conversation, ready to do all good offices to his friends, and charitable to the poor almost beyond his ability.'

The person who supplied the MS of the 'Thanksgivings' for publication was probably Susanna Hopton, a learned lady and devout Christian, some ten years older than Traherne, who was the central figure in a religious group, meeting at her house in Kington, some fifteen miles from Credenhill. It has been thought that Traherne was a member of this group, and that his major work, the 'Centuries of Meditations' was addressed to Susanna. There is no definite proof of this: what is certain is that Traherne gained inspiration from, and gave instruction to, a woman friend, and that much of the special quality of the Centuries derives from its being addressed to a person. The dedication is 'to the friend of my best friend' who has given him the notebook, and after filling it with 'profitable wonders' he is to return it to her so that she may 'write my Maker's praise' on the blank pages remaining at the end of the book.

At some date as yet uncertain, Traherne left his parish (though remaining nominally its Rector until his death) for a more sophisticated setting, where his learning and powers of disputation would be exercised. His patron was a distinguished lawyer, Sir Orlando Bridgeman, Lord Keeper of the Privy Seal, until he was deprived of it for his obstinacy in refusing to employ it on Indulgences and on grants to Charles II's mistresses. He lived at Essex House in the Strand and at Teddington in Middlesex, where Traherne continued his ministry. Probably at this time Traherne prepared his one formal work of Christian teaching, published in the year after he died: 'Christian Ethicks; or, Divine Morality: opening the Way to Blessedness, by the Rules of Virtue and Reason.' And here, in 'the Lady Bridgeman's house at Teddington' as his Will has it, he died, at the early age of 37, leaving his best hat and his books to his brother Philip, then in Turkey, and making Philip and Philip's wife Susan (who was present) executors of the Will. Orlando Bridgeman had predeceased his chaplain in June of that year.

Although Traherne was so eager to convey his news of Felicity to contemporaries, he took little care for posterity, and the disappearance of his writings after his death, with their haphazard rediscovery in our century, makes one of the oddest of textual histories. Apart from the two works mentioned, he left his writings not only unpublished, but unsigned as well. As a result, poems by William Austin and Francis Quarles, written in a notebook among poems of his own, came to be included as his when his Collected Poems were published in our own day.[4]

Both the anonymous 'Thanksgivings' and 'Christian Ethics' were forgotten, and no one suspected that a major seventeenth-century writer remained to be discovered, until the literary acumen and flair of a bookseller, Bertram Dobell, identified Traherne as the author (at first thought to be Henry Vaughan) of a manuscript collection picked up on a second-hand bookstall for a few pence by his friend W. T. Brooke. Shortly afterwards Dobell bought the notebook which contains the Centuries of Meditations, and published these and the poems in editions with modernised spellings: later on he acquired other notebooks. Ten years after the first announcement of the poems, another manuscript of poems was located in the British Library by Sir Idris Bell, when he was looking among the Burney Papers for something else: it had Thomas Traherne's name on the title-page, though it was in the handwriting of Philip.

The poems from all notebooks, the prose Centuries, and the Thanksgivings, were published in 1958 in a scholarly edition by H. M. Margoliouth. But more surprises were in store. In the 1960s John Hayward, deputed by the American bibliophile James Osborn to look out for interesting items for sale, noticed the description 'Centuries of Meditations' in a bookseller's catalogue, and this, duly acquired, turned out to be another notebook, not in Traherne's handwriting but clearly of his authorship: now known as 'Select Meditations', it is still unpublished. Strangest of all was the accident (in 1967) that rescued from a bonfire another Traherne manuscript in verse and prose. For an account of both these discoveries, turn to Julia Smith's article.

Considering this tale of happy accidents, it seems more than possible that further manuscripts may come to light – perhaps a further volume of Philip Traherne's transcription of the poems, for the one we have is marked Volume I. But I feel that we could hardly know more of Traherne's thought than we do, so vividly has he expressed his essential vision. It is a vision of paradise, existing here and now, not only in Vaughan's 'country Far beyond the stars'. *Paradise*, we should say, but Traherne calls it Felicity, which was also Edmund Spenser's word. ('And grant that we, for whom thou diddest die...May live for ever in Felicity'[5].) To know this paradise is to be in eternity, which is like a sphere into which we enter. God placed Man at the centre of the world so that he might fully contemplate it (as Traherne quotes from Pico della Mirandola), but also, Man carries Paradise within himself: he knows Felicity *now*, not putting it off until some future state. Though some Christians do this, and set their hopes on happiness in an after-life, Traherne thinks they are to be suspected, for 'it is against the Nature of Lov and desire to defer'. (*Centuries* IV, 9) To walk in such a paradise, to contain such a paradise, is a matter of man's free choice (IV, 80):

> By chusing a Man may be turned and Converted into Lov. Which as it is an Universal Sun filling and shining in the Eternity of GOD, so is it infinitly more Glorious then the Sun is, not only shedding abroad more Amiable and Delightfull Beams, Illuminating and Comforting all Objects...but is of all sensibles the most Quick and Tender; being able to feel like the longlegged Spider at the utmost End of its Divaricated feet: and to be wholy present in every place where any Beam of itself extends...And of all Beings such a Being would I chuse to be for ever.

Traherne is so filled with the energy of this vision, that one feels he had to give it speech whether he would or no — an Ancient Mariner, but impelled by joy not guilt. The prose paragraph form of the *Centuries* and *Christian Ethics* seems exactly suited to his genius, giving him scope to range freely in imagination over a wide range of objects, yet imposing a light restraint. In poetry (where he explores the same themes), although he does sometimes achieve the perfect expression of his thought, he is too voluble, generally too impatient a craftsman, to be among the greatest, and the elaborate stanza forms he uses (never repeating the pattern exactly from poem to poem) often seem merely to constrain the thought he must cram into them.

Christian Ethics has magnificent passages, and shows Traherne as more deliberately a moralist than in his *Centuries*. (An edition with modernized spelling was edited by Margaret Bottrall in 1962, with the more attractive part of its full title, 'The Way to Blessedness'.) The exposition of his purpose with which it opens might serve for all his works. His aim, he says,

> is not to stroke and tickle the fancy but to elevate the soul and refine its apprehensions, to inform the judgment and polish it for conversation (that is, interchange with others in the fullest sense), to purify and enflame the heart, to enrich the mind, and guide men that stand in need of help in the way of virtue; to excite their desire, to encourage

them to travel, to comfort them in the journey, and so at last to lead them to true Felicity, both here and hereafter.[6]

A magnificent statement of intent – and note that although the subject is morals, men's hearts are to be enflamed and their desire excited. But as I have said, the fact that the *Centuries* were addressed to a person, gives them their special vitality, and where the argument is reinforced by personal recollection, there is a radiance in the prose unmatched elsewhere. The MS we have is not a fair copy: Traherne is composing on to the page, sometimes deleting a passage, or substituting words or phrases. The title 'Centuries of Meditations' was added by a later hand, and although Traherne has numbered the paragraphs from the beginning, he does not use the word *Century* till after the first hundred. The frequent repetition of words and phrases, which can be wearisome if you read much at a time, is a necessary part of the method. Louis Martz traces its ancestry to St Augustine, with a philosophical basis in the effort to reach the unapprehended Platonic Ideal by conjuring up the forms of things already known. He quotes a passage from Augustine which exactly describes this method:

What is this thing capable of form but still unformed, but a process in our mind, darting hither and thither with a kind of movement of passage, as we turn our thought from one object to another in the course of discovery or presentation? It becomes a true word, only when what I have called this darting movement of passage comes upon what we know[what was stored in our memory but still undefined] and takes form from it...[7]

For example, Traherne in his First Century plays a kind of extravaganza on ways of enjoying (or as we might say valuing) the world, leading to the truth that to enjoy it you must love it as God loves it – and that to love it is to possess it.

There *is* a discernible shape and sequence to both *Christian Ethics* and the *Centuries*, though it is hard to keep in mind as one reads. A very brief summary of the *Centuries* would run thus. After expounding his purpose to his correspondent, teaching her to enjoy and so possess the world, Traherne meditates on the mystery of the Cross and God's love, ending with prayers to Christ. The Second Century resumes the subject of rightly possessing the world, which leads to a superb sequence on the nature of Love, and of the soul. The Third Century illustrates the way to discover Felicity by examples from the writer's own life, and then studies the Psalms, as showing the nature of God and our relation to him. The Fourth Century expounds some twenty principles of knowing Felicity; and the Fifth (which has only ten paragraphs) describes Eternity, and shows that Felicity is a union of God and the soul.

Many aspects of Traherne's teaching can be matched with those of other thinkers of his time. Affinities with the Cambridge Platonists have been pointed out, especially with the *Discourses* of John Smith. He too lays emphasis on man's capacity for goodness, in contrast with the Puritan stress on his predisposition to sin. Yet if you read the *Discourses*, you find that an account of blessedness is generally balanced by a 'Whereas on the contrary wicked men...' much more rarely found in Traherne; and he lacks Traherne's confidence in the whole man, writing for instance: 'The soul seems to be ashamed that it should be in the body.'

Moreover, Traherne looks at the world with the eye of a poet, and he is with Henry Vaughan among the small number (stretching from Dante through Wordsworth to Edwin Muir) who exalt the holiness of the child's perception: exalt it, and at moments retrieve it. Most people retrieve this way of seeing only when they fall in love, like Tolstoy's Levin in *Anna Karenina*:

> What he then saw he never saw again. Two children going to school, some pigeons that flew down from the roof, and a few loaves put outside a baker's window...All of these things were so unusually beautiful that Levin laughed and cried with joy[8].

In this context I am reminded of a remarkable Romanes lecture by Kenneth Clark entitled 'Moments of Vision'[9], a phrase he applies not to prophetic writings, 'whose authors have usually felt that things which a man can see with his own eyes were not sufficiently awe-inspiring to be communications of the divine', but to those 'flashes' when familiar objects are seen in the light of eternity. And these experiences, which we all had in childhood (whether we can recall them or not), he relates to a collective memory. He quotes this illuminating passage from Coleridge:

In looking at objects of nature...as at yonder moon dim glimmering through the dewy window pane, I seem rather to be seeking a symbolic language for something within me that forever and already exists, than observing anything new. Even when that latter is the case, yet still I have always an obscure feeling, as if that new phenomenon were a dim awakening of a forgotten or hidden truth of my inner nature.[10]

This last phrase links up with the passage I quoted earlier from Augustine about the process of thought. Now Clark, in trying to analyse *why* these moments cause us so much joy, concludes that it is because the object seen, while remaining truly itself, is possessed by us. 'We possess it, and are possessed by it.' Such a phrase immediately reminds him of Traherne, and especially of those passages from the Third Century which are the ones everyone remembers.

The Corn was Orient and Immortal Wheat, which never should be reaped, nor was ever sown. I thought it had stood from Everlasting to Everlasting. The Dust and Stones of the Street were as precious as GOLD. The Gates were at first the End of the World, The Green Trees when I saw them first through one of the Gates Transported and Ravished me; their Sweetness and unusual Beauty made my Heart to leap, and almost mad with Extasie, they were such strange and Wonderfull Thing(s); The Men! O what venerable and Reverend Creatures did the Aged seem! Immortal Cherubims! And yong men Glittering Sparkling Angels and Maids strange Seraphick Pieces of Life and Beauty! Boys and Girles Tumbling in the Street, and Playing, were moving Jewels. I knew not that they were Born or should Die. But all things abided Eternaly as they were in their Proper Places. Eternity was Manifest in the Light of the Day, and som thing infinit Behind evry thing appeared: which talked with my Expectation and moved my Desire. The Citie seemed to stand in Eden, or to be Built in Heaven. The Streets were mine, the Temple was mine, the People were mine, their Clothes and Gold and Silver was mine, as much as their Sparkling Eys fair Skins and ruddy faces. (III, 3)

A few paragraphs further on Traherne includes a poem, 'News from a forrein Country came', which expresses the same ideas. It is a fine poem, and the only one of his to be chosen by successive editors of the Oxford Book of English Verse. But of all his poems on infancy, my favourites are 'Shadows in the Water' and its companion 'On Leaping over the Moon'.

In unexperienc'd Infancy
Many a sweet Mistake doth ly:
Mistake tho false, intending tru;
A *Seeming* somwhat more than *View*;
That doth instruct the Mind
In Things that ly behind,
And many Secrets to us show
Which afterwards we com to know.

Thus did I by the Water's brink
Another World beneath me think;
And while the lofty spacious Skies
Reversed there abus'd mine Eyes,
I fancy'd other Feet
Came mine to touch and meet;
As by some Puddle I did play
Another World within it lay.

The metaphysical implications of reflections in water fascinated him, and here he takes the child's literal view, and ambiguous sense of scale, which Lewis Carroll exploited in the 'Alice' books (as also Marvell in 'Upon Appleton House'), and leads by this means to his favourite conclusion:

...below the purling Stream
Som unknown Joys there be
Laid up in Store for me;
To which I shall, when that thin Skin
Is broken, be admitted in.

Many Christians who first read Traherne in their youth must surely find him as marvellously liberating as I did; a counter-balance to the distrust of the body (and especially of the sexual instincts) prevalent in much of Christian teaching – the implication that in the loss of Eden 'the body had somehow fallen farther than the soul', as Charles Williams put it. And for those who try to find their way to God in everyday life, the saying of St John of the Cross, 'Hence the soul cannot be possessed of the divine union until it has divested itself of the love of created beings', can lie across the path like the flaming sword that barred Adam from Paradise.

Now no doubt the distinction between *attachment* and *detach-*

ment, both of them distinct from *indifference*, is relevant here; nevertheless Traherne's emphasis on 'the holiness of the heart's affections' (Keats's phrase) is a talisman against wasteful guilt and self-doubt.

You are as Prone to lov, as the Sun is to shine. It being the most Delightfull and Natural Employment of the Soul of Man: without which you are Dark and Miserable. Consider therefore the Extent of Lov, its Vigor and Excellency. For certainly He that Delights not in Lov makes vain the Univers, and is of Necessity to Himself the Greatest Burden...

That Violence wherewith somtimes a man doteth upon one Creature, is but a little spark of that lov, even towards all, which lurketh in His Nature. We are made to lov: both to satisfy the Necessity of our Activ Nature, and to answer the Beauties in evry Creature. By Lov our souls are married and sodderd to the creatures: and it is our Duty like God to be united to them all. We must lov them infinitly but in God, and for God: and God in them. When we dote upon the Perfections and Beauties of som one Creature: we do not lov that too much, but other things too little. Never was any thing in this World loved too much, but many Things have been loved in a fals Way: and all in too short a Measure.

Lov is so vastly Delightfull in the Lover, becaus it is the Communication of His Goodness; for the Natural End of Goodness is to be Enjoyed: it Desireth to be anothers Happiness. Which Goodness of GOD is so deeply implanted in our Natures, that we never Enjoy our selvs but when we are the Joy of others: of all our Desires the Strongest is to be Good to others. We Delight in Receiving, more in Giving. We lov to be Rich: but then it is, that we thereby might be more Greatly Delightfull; thus we see the Seeds of Eternity Sparkling in our Natures. (II, 65, 66, 57)

'He that delights not in Love, makes vain the Universe'. Such aphorisms remain in the mind, even though we are sometimes overwhelmed by the accumulation of instances and comparisons. One such occurs in another fine passage on Love, where Traherne maintains with his usual good sense that we cannot love others unless we first love ourselves: 'That pool must first be filled, that shall be made to overflow.' (IV, 55)

I have praised Traherne for his freedom from the oppressive sense of guilt that can taint Christian attitudes. Some have blamed him for a defective sense of sin – even a facile optimism. And when he writes that 'of all our desires the strongest is to be good to others', he provokes a wry smile, as we look into our own souls, or indeed at the casual selfishness apparent in our streets and supermarkets. Yet that optimism must have been dearly won. Here is a man who had lost his parents early, whose childhood was passed during the civil war with all its cruelties, who had known his king cruelly executed. Every now and then in the notebooks one sees a glimpse of depression and distress but, as with Oliver Edwards in Boswell's Life of Johnson, cheerfulness was always breaking in.

I do not wish to dwell on the passage that so horrified Dobell, where Traherne, following Aquinas and other Church Fathers, says that the Happy must enjoy the thought of Hell, as part of God's world – 'his Prison'. (I, 48) Coming on such a saying, from the gentle Traherne, one can only echo Lear's question to Cordelia, 'But goes thy heart with this?' To understand the true nature of his optimism, we do better to study his meditations on the Cross in the First Century. Ecstatic praises of the Cross (the Abyss of Wonders, the Centre of Desires...the Root of Happiness, and the Gate of Heaven') give way to the contemplation of Christ's sufferings, and the paradox that these should be cause of rejoicing:

> Can this be a Joy...Can this Delight us...Thou wast slain for me: and shall I leav thy Body in the feild O Lord? Shall I go away and be Merry, while the Love of my Soul and my only Lover is Dead upon the Cross? (I, 89)

The answer lies in the nature of God's love for us: a love that has raised us out of nothing, and made us the heirs of all the ages: this is the wellspring of Traherne's confidence in Felicity.

> GOD never shewd himself more a GOD, then when He appeared Man. Never gained more Glory then when he lost all Glory. Was never more Sensible of our Sad Estate, then when he was bereaved of all Sence...This Sampson by dying Kild all His Enemies: And then carried the Gates of Hell and Death away, when being Dead, Himself was born to his Grave. (I, 90)

Notes

1. *The Paradise Within*, New Haven & London 1964, p.83
2. Quoted by Margaret Bottrall, *The Prayers of Thomas Traherne*, Cambridge 1988, p.21
3. Quoted by James Osborn, *Times Literary Supplement*, 8.10.64
4. See my Preface to the Oxford Standard Authors edition of Traherne, 1966
5. from 'Easter'
6. Quoted from Margaret Bottrall's edition, London 1962, p.17
7. *The Paradise Within*, op.cit. p.49
8. *Anna Karenina,* Oxford University Press 1937, p.52
9. *Moments of Vision*, Clarendon Press 1964
10. op.cit. p.16

The Sacrifice of Praise and Thanksgiving

A. M. ALLCHIN

Returning to the study of Traherne after some time away from him, I have found myself increasingly impressed by the idea that he is a writer who has a very particular message for our own day. It is clear that there is much about him still to be discovered.

In saying this I do not want to suggest that he was not a man of his own time. It will be the basic thesis of this essay that he was not only a man of startling and original poetic vision, but also a man of tradition, a convinced and articulate representative of the theological and spiritual view-point of the Church of which he was a minister. Part of his importance for us lies in the way in which he holds together different elements which are often thought to be in opposition to one another, the specific vision of childhood, a love for the Church's tradition, a keen and enquiring intellect.

In this very unity, he is a man of his own century. Onc of the fascinations of the seventeenth century for us lies in the way in which its people held together things which later became dissociated. As David Cecil writes of the men and women of that age 'Their existence was far more integrated than ours. They felt no awkward dissonance between the ideal and the real, the poetic and the prosaic. They did not distinguish between a man's public and his private personality. Accepting equally the earthly and the heavenly, their vision embraced all experience in one harmony. They wrote a lyric, and called on the name of God, and went to law about a will with the same unembarrassed wholeheartedness'.[1]

Traherne is known today above all for the 'Centuries of Meditations', and for the passages in them which speak so powerfully of the vision of a transfigured world, a world in which eternity seems present in time, and time is held within the grasp of eternity. 'Eternity was Manifest in the Light of the Day, and som thing infinit Behind every thing appeared: which talked with my Expectation and moved my Desire'.[2]

That vision has beeen expressed a number of times in the last two centuries. William Wordsworth is perhaps its greatest exponent. In our own time Edwin Muir has spoken of it in his poems and in the opening chapters of his autobiography. More surprisingly perhaps Eugene Ionesco witnesses to its significance for him. I myself lived and worked for nine years with someone for whom the memory of that vision was a constant reality; I know how deeply it can influence a person's whole attitude towards life. Hugh Maycock was sustained throughout his life by his memory of a childhood experience of Eden. In the very last sermon which he preached at the convent of Burwash, he quoted at length from Traherne's poem 'The Salutation'.

Is that first vision of a world full of the divine glory something given only to a few, or is it something which we all have had? I incline to think that it is a common possession, though in the case of most of us one so deeply buried as to be beyond conscious recall. But something in us resonates to the description of it when we hear of it from others.

Among Traherne's contemporaries, one who expressed that vision not so insistently as Traherne, but in a quite unmistakable way, was Henry Vaughan[3]. Henry Vaughan and Thomas Traherne were contemporaries. But whereas the former lived seventy-four years, from 1621 to 1695, the latter lived just half that time from 1637 to 1674. We have no knowledge as to whether they ever met, but they shared much in their attitudes to religious and political questions. Henry Vaughan lived in the valley of the Usk and lies buried at Llansantffraed, about thirty miles from Hereford. In the seventeenth century his was a solidly Welsh-speaking area, and we know that Henry Vaughan's first language was Welsh.

As to Traherne we have no evidence that he knew Welsh. But the Welsh language line came to within five miles of Hereford in his time, and many of the parishes in the west of the county were Welsh speaking. The Bishop of Hereford was included with the four Welsh bishops in the royal commission to supervise the Welsh edition of the 1662 Prayer Book. If Traherne did not know Welsh, he must at least have known of the existence of Welsh.

The language was constantly heard in the streets of Hereford on market days. He was born and brought up on the frontier of a people in whose tradition, whether he knew of it or not, the work of the poet is understood above all else as the work of praise, praise of God in and through a transfigured world. That was evidently how he understood his calling.

Traherne was a man of original vision and at the same time a representative of a whole tradition. Similarly he was a man who felt a deep need for solitude and at the same time had a great love of company. In one of his Thanksgivings he says 'Thou Lord hast made thy servant a sociable creature; for which I praise thy name; a lover of company; a delighter in equals; replenish the inclination which thyself hast implanted'.[4] He had a longing to communicate the vision which he had received and to share it with others. He seems to have been tireless both in talk and in writing.

He grew up at a time when the use of the Book of Common Prayer was forbidden by law. He was educated at Brasenose during the Commonwealth; it was a college of strong Puritan sympathies. He was appointed to the benefice of Credenhill in 1657 on the recommendation of some of the leading Puritan figures of the county. He must at that time have been acceptable to them. He had therefore to *become* an Anglican by conscious choice. The early date of his episcopal ordination in 1660 provides evidence that he was anxious to do this. This was more than a matter of complying with a legal requirement. As we shall see he became a great lover of the Book of Common Prayer and of the whole tradition of liturgical worship which it conveyed. These were not things which he grew up with.

Our principal source of knowledge about Traherne in this area is the little manuscript book in the Bodleian Library, which has been known since the beginning of this century and to which Margoliouth gave the title 'The Church's Year Book'. It is a book of meditations and prayers which covers the period from Easter to All Saints Day. Was it one of a pair? We do not know. At least we may be thankful that this book has survived, giving us, as it does, Traherne's thoughts for Easter and Ascension and Pentecost, and for the week before Pentecost which he calls 'the

Week of Expectation', no less than for saint's days like St John the Baptist and St Peter, for All Saints and Michaelmas.

Though known since the beginning of the century, the manuscript has never been published. From the literary point of view it is of unequal value, and in some ways frustrating. At least half of the contents are quoted or adapted, or summarised from others, usually without acknowledgement. Yet it is not just a commonplace book. As Carol Marks, the American scholar who has worked most on it, remarks, 'despite the manifold debts, it bears the stamp of his own wisdom'. This is largely due 'to Traherne's persistent, if maddening habit of assimilating to his own manner and thought the style and ideas of other writers'.[5]

What is maddening from the point of view of the literary scholar, may be fascinating and even helpful from the point of view of someone trying to understand Traherne not only as an original writer, but also as a representative of a Church, and of a particular school of thought within that Church. Of course one is pleased when one can identify passages as distinctly his own. But the passages which he quotes, or more often adapts from others are also highly significant. We want to see what it is and who it is that has attracted him. Throughout the book we find a man assimilating a tradition in such a way as to be assimilated by it, making an anthology in order to stimulate and inform his prayer and his understanding of his faith.

As soon as we begin to enumerate the writers whose work he cites, we see that he is appealing to the classical Anglican teachers of his time. In the meditations after Easter he makes use of the Easter sermons of Lancelot Andrewes. In the reflections for Michaelmas he cites both Hooker and Andrewes on the subject of angels. He quotes prayers from Jeremy Taylor and a poem of George Herbert's. He makes use of two earlier books of devotion, those of Daniel Fealtry (1626) and William Austin (1635), and of two commentaries on the Book of Common Prayer published during the Commonwealth, Edward Sparke (1652) and Anthony Sparrow (1655). Many of his patristic and medieval quotations have come through them. Traherne was a man of wide and varied reading, rather than an original scholar. We do not know when the manuscript was written. On the strength of internal evidence it has usually been attributed to Traherne's later years at Teddington. The evidence seems to be less than conclusive. It might as well be a work of the period immediately after the restoration. It is interesting that none of the sources identified by Carol Marks dates from after 1660.

The title given to the book 'The Church's Year Book', though not Traherne's own, is highly appropriate. The book is an exposition of and meditation on the feasts of the Church's year and of the whole way of worship of which those feasts are a part. It is necessarily to some extent defensive, and occasionally even polemical, since it is constantly touching on points at issue between the upholders of the Book of Common Prayer and all that it implied for the Church's tradition of faith and prayer on the one side, and those who opposed them on the other.

The very observance of the traditional festivals was a cause of contention. By what authority do we keep the feast of Christmas for instance? It is clearly not enjoined in the Scripture. Indeed the feast was instituted by the Church in Rome to respond to a pagan mid-winter festival. Has the Church the right to establish such celebrations? To those who worked with a rigid interpretation of the rule *Sola Scriptura*, it was clear that Christmas and the whole cycle of feasts to which it belonged had no place in a reformed Church.

Traherne, of course, follows the Anglican appeal to Scripture as interpreted through tradition with the aid of reason. As long as nothing is established against the Scriptures, we may rightly follow the tradition of the Church, for as Article XX states 'The Church hath power to decree Rites or Ceremonies and authority in Controversies of Faith'. And for him, the Church now, despite the break with Rome, is continuous with the Church before the reformation, as we see very clearly in the passage about the little church surrounded by trees, which is quoted in the Appendix. So Traherne defends not only the feasts of our Lord, but also those of the apostles, the evangelists, St Stephen and the Holy Innocents, the angels and All Saints, all of them major celebrations in the Book of Common Prayer.

These questions were for Traherne by no means purely formal or external matters. The feast-days provided ways in which he could rediscover and re-appropriate his childhood vision of a world in which time was held in the embrace of eternity, in which eternity was present in the midst of time. They were ways in which he could unite what was most private and personal to himself, with what was commonly recognised and publicly authorised. They were also, as we shall see, ways in which he could link the liturgy which took place inside the church building with the sanctification of the world around it. As a child he had seen the world transfigured. He knew instinctively that there were holy times and holy places. He found confirmation of these intuitions in the liturgical faith and practice of the Church.

It is not difficult to imagine that for Traherne there was a particular problem in discovering how to relate the religion of creation with its apprehension of the innocence of childhood on the one side, with the religion of redemption with its stress on the totality of the fall of man on the other. In 'The Centuries' we can see with what delight he discovered the elements in the psalms which speak of God's glory as revealed in creation, and of creation's part in responding to God with praise and thanksgiving (III sections 66 - 94). In his almost ecstatic rehearsal of these strands in the prayer of the Old Testament, we can see how vital it was for Traherne to find both in Scripture and tradition the roots and the relatedness of his personal vision.

It is particularly interesting that in one of the passages where he speaks of the rightness of observing holy seasons as well as recognising holy places, he refers to the transfiguration on Mount Tabor. At this time the feast of the Transfiguration was only a black letter day in the Book of Common Prayer. It had no active celebration and consequently does not have a treatment of its own in Traherne's meditations. But the reference to it is there in a passage whose significance is underlined by the use of capitals in the original text. 'For, if such a memorable Action as our Savior's Transfiguration upon Mount Tabor, shall make it even by S. Peter himself to be called in the New Testament THE HOLY MOUNT, well may such Memorable and Divine Occurrences as the Resurrection of our Savior, and the Giving of the Holy Ghost make the Times wherein they came to pass both called and esteemed HOLY TIMES. Since Times as well as Places are capable of the impression of HOLY THINGS'.[6]

This reflection occurs in a meditation on the coming of the Holy Spirit. It forms part of Traherne's understanding of the sacramental character of the work of our redemption in which God constantly makes use of material things to act in this world, and in which the whole of that redemptive work is brought to completion by the coming of the Holy Spirit, who carries up our human nature into union with the divine nature. Again creation and redemption are being held together, again the transfiguration of Christ, no less than his baptism, is seen as a manifestation of the Trinity.

Therefore in Baptism doth God use Water to signifie the Washing away of Spiritual pollutions, in the Lord's Supper Bread and Wine, to signifie the Divine and Eternal feast whereof we are by the Body and Blood of Christ made joynt Partakers. And therefore in the Old Law He exhibited Himself under the Elements of Oyl, Water and fire, as in the Baptism of Christ He took upon himself the form of a Dove, to signifie the Innocencie and fecundity of Good Works, in those whom He Inspireth, as well as his own Meek and Excellent Nature. In the Transfiguration of Christ, He appeareth like a Transplendent Cloud, to signifie the Dew and Rain of Holy Doctrine which He communicateth. In the Supping Chamber He was given by Christ as a Breath in sign of the Spiritual Life he bestoweth, but this Day, He appeared in the form of fire; for there appeared to them Cloven Tongues as it were of fire, and it sate upon each of them. Because as fire is the Most Bright and Activ of Bodies, the Holy Ghost is the most Living and Glorious of Beings: as fire doth Enlighten, purifie, kindle, carry up on High, is in itself very Unitiv, Transforming into itself, that which is conjoyned to it, and wholly communicativ; so the Holy Ghost doth Enlighten the understanding, purifie souls, consume the Rust of Sins and Imperfections, Enkindle the Will with Divine Lov, ever flaming to God in pious Affections, Holy Devotions and pure Adorations, and to our Neighbour in Upright and pious Actions. It doth elevat Hearts from Earthly to Heavenly Things, and caus it [sic] to Repose in Heaven its Natural Seat, by Divine Contemplations; it doth unite the Soul with God, and communicat His Gifts and vertues to the Soul, in such a Manner that they become one Spirit, by the Union of perfect Lov.[7]

Already here and now, through the action of the Holy Spirit, bringing to completion the saving work of Christ, we are made one with God, and in the life of the Church begin to enter into the Kingdom of eternity.

It is this present participation in the joys of heaven which the

Church's feast days are intended to celebrate and proclaim, and Traherne reflects on this in a passage where he speaks of the beauty of holy days considered in themselves. In order to express his sense of the richness and mystery of sacred times and seasons, Traherne employs a particular form of his method of repetition, piling image on image, in order to fill out his vision of these spots of time as restorations of Eden and anticipations of heaven.

Why should we not spend som time upon Holy Days in Contemplating the Beauty of Holy Dais in themselves?
They are the Ornaments of Time, and the Beauty of the World.
The Days of Heaven seen upon Earth,
The Seasons of Melody, Joy and Thanksgiving.
The Lucid Intervals and Lights of the Year,
The Relicks of Eden, and superadded Treasures,
A gratefull Relaxation from Cares and Labors.
The very Cream and Crown and Repose of our Lives...
Wherein we Antedate the Resurrection of the Dead
And come from our shops to our Saviour's Throne,
From plowing our feilds to Manna in the Wilderness,
From Dressing our Vineyards to the Wine of Angels
From Caring for our Children to be the Sons of God.
They are Heavenly Perspectivs wherein we behold the Mystery of the Ages.
Spiritual Regions, wherein we Walk in the paths of GOD.
Market Days of Heaven,
Appointed Seasons, wherein GOD keepeth Open House
And Blessed Opportunities wherein we com from our solitary Closets and see ourselvs in Solemn Assemblies.
Single Devotions are weak in comparison of these; here is the Joy and the Strength of Union.
A Privat Person is but Half Himself, and naturally magnified in others.
He is enlarged and Multiplied, when he sees Himself in so many faces in Divine Assemblies.
The Difference between Earth and Heaven is, that here we are Dispersed, there we shall ever be united together.
These Days are Tastes and Earnests of our Eternal Rest,
Wherein we enter the Temple, as the Schole of Christ
And like Angels are adorned with Wings
That we might flie unto heaven.
Wherein like Brides we are prepaired with Ornaments

That we might Enjoy the Bridegroom of our Souls in Glory.
O my God, they are Mysterious Opportunities, Diffusing our Souls and Elevating them to Heaven.
Landskips of Glory
Golden Links uniting our Souls and All Things together.
Apostles, King David and Solomon entertain us.
Saints and Martyrs visit us.
Without Contemplation we lose the Benefit of Ages, and without such Days the Benefit of Contemplation.
The King's Exchequer is laid open, and the Doors are open into all His Treasures.
Without Sanctifying these we lose the Benefit and the End of our lives, which is to enter into the Treasuries of GOD Almighty, and to feel his Lov, and to offer up ourselves in Joy and Thanksgivings.
What Strangers are they to this Kingdom that are Disputers against it? How much are their Palats vitiated that cannot Delight in Such Heavenly Banquets!'[8]

The seventeenth century Anglican teachers did not believe that it was right to address the saints directly in prayer. They felt that they had no warrant in Scripture for the practice, and that to 'pray' to the saints ran the risk of offering to creatures the worship duc to the Creator alone. Traherne quotes George Herbert's poem on this subject in its entirety.[9] But this did not mean that they regarded the article of faith in the communion of saints, as of little importance. Granted this limitation, they were prepared to say much about the way in which the saints on earth and the saints beyond the boundary of death are united in their common worship of the one God. Indeed Traherne does not hesitate to say that we are in contact with them through their relics and the places where they are buried.

In a qualified sense, the very Bodies of Saints are held sacred by us, and used venerably of us, being gathered to their fathers, and Honorably Disposed of into Quiet Graves.

For they were once Temples of the living God,
They were the Storehouses of His Holy Word
The Earthen Vessels of Heavenly Treasures,
The Living Conduit-Pipes of the Holy Ghost,
The Members of our Savior's Bodie
The Reliques of Celestial Kings
The Seeds of Eternity

Whom Nature teacheth us to handle with respect.
As we see in the very Heathen, who scarce knew the Immortality of the Soul, yet thought it highly Dreadfull not to cover the Members of the Dead, and with Sacred Reverence Deposited their Ashes in Honorable Urns.
Those that contemn the Buriall of the Dead, quickly contemn all things venerable and honorable among men.
They need not our Prayers being already Happy.
Neither need we Invocat them having free Access unto the
    Throne of Grace,
Yet we reverance and Commemorat them,
We prais God for them,
We Contemplat their Lives,
We Imitat their Virtues
We Glory in their Crowns
We rejoyce in the felicity of His Chosen.
It is our Duty to GOD
Our Honor of them,
A Benefit to our Selvs
A communion of Saints with the Saints of all ages.
It is a Grand Novelty and Ingratitude to do otherwise.[10]

And we remember that for Traherne, ingratitude is one of the gravest of all sins.

It is in the context of this celebration of the communion of saints, that we must place the meditation on Mary, which is one of the very few passages from 'The Church's Year Book' to have been published so far. Since we do not have the book which would have included the feasts of the Purification or the Annunciation, the two Marian feasts observed as red letter days in the Church of England at that time, we do not know what Traherne would have made of them. It is however highly significant that here he places his thoughts about Mary within the context of the consideration of the saints in general. It is within that fellowship that Anglicans have loved to think of her.

And first O Lord I praise and magnifie thy Name
For the Most Holy Virgin-Mother of God, who is the Highest of
    thy Saints.
The most Glorious of all thy Creatues.
The most Perfect of all thy Works.
The nearest unto Thee, in the Throne of God.

Traherne goes on to apply to Mary many beautiful titles, concluding the first part of his meditation with the words: 'The most Illustrious Light in the Church, Wearing over all her Beauties the veil of Humility to shine the more resplendently in thy Eternal Glory.'[11]

The terms in which Traherne praises Mary are certainly exuberant, but I see no reason to suppose, as some have suggested, that he borrowed this material from a Roman Catholic source. Rather his text reveals a very typical Anglican dialectic, acknowledging first the uniqueness of Mary's calling, and then placing her within the company of the saints and angels who all alike worship God. The piling up of images and titles parallels exactly the lists of epithets which we have seen applied to the saints in general and to holy days themselves.

But for Traherne the appointed celebrations of the Church's year are not only a way by which our minds are lifted up to heaven. They are also a way in which our daily life and labour is sanctified. This is especially true in the case of the Rogation Days, the days of prayer for God's blessing on the fields and crops which are observed in the week leading up to Ascension Day. Here again, we can observe him both as a typical spokesman for the Church of England in his day, and also as one who has a particular concern to link the worship of the Church on Sunday with the hallowing of the world of nature, so that the fields around the church, no less than the church building itself can be recognised as forming the house of God.

In particular in his meditations on these days we see his wholehearted belief in the unity of the church and the nation, and in the conjunction of sacred and secular. For him, as for Hooker, church and kingdom are two sides of the same reality. After the experiences of the Commonwealth, people had to choose between the idea of the 'gathered Church' on the one side, and the idea of the national Church on the other. There can be no question where Traherne stands on this issue. We also see in these lines an expression of his basic belief that we realise our true wealth, not by clinging to our private possessions, but by recognising the gifts of God which are common to all, and valuing them aright.

So on such days of prayer we learn 'to be affected with the

great and Publick Concernments of the Nation and Kingdom in which we Liv, espousing the Benefit and Welfare of all.' To do this

> will giv us a Communion with GOD Almighty in all His publick Ways and Blessings, Mercies and Judgements, His People's Joys, His Glorious Works which are abroad in the World.
>
> And certainly in this the Wisdom of the Church is infinit, for she leadeth us in the Circuit of all his Mercies. And having upon other Holy Days brought us by Degrees to Things Past ... she now leads us by the Hand to the Sight and Possession of Temporal Delights and Earthly Blessings, even to present Affairs in the Dispensations of His Providence, and the Visible Beauties of His Works Beneath, which in their proper season come also to be Remembered, for it is not Gold and Silver, and the Things in our Houses that will make us Happy, without a lively sight and sense of the Benefits which he hath prepared abroad, and by giving which He hath magnified the Greatness of his Wisdom and Lov.
>
> They have ordained also Procession at this Time, to view and Secure the Publick Bounds, which is an Act of Justice, being a Fence against Wrong, an Act of Prudence in Removing Trouble; an Act of Charity by preventing Quarrels. And to Compleat all they have made it an Act of Thanksgiving by Joyning his Praises to so Convenient a Season, and an Act of Triumph and Publick Joy in Causing the Minister to go abroad with his People in Token and Memory of the victory of Christians ...[12]

In his commendation of the Rogation-tide procession around the fields, for the beating of the bounds, Traherne is following directly in the line of George Herbert as he describes it in 'The Country Parson'. 'The Country Parson is a Lover of old Customes, if they be good and harmless; and the rather, because Country People are much addicted to them ... Particularly, he loves Procession, and maintains it.' Herbert adds to Traherne's reasons for approving this custom, two more, 'Charity in loving walking, and neighbourly accompanying one another, with reconciling of differences at that time, if there be any' and, 'Mercy, in relieving the poor by a liberall distribution and largesse, which at that time is, or ought to be used'.[13] We have no direct evidence for the nature of Traherne's pastoral ministry during the years in which he resided at Credenhill, but we may be certain that Herbert's prose work was as familiar to him as his poems were. Both writers breathe that respect and affection for the ordinary, daily customs of village life, which accords well with their anxious concern for the good of society as a whole, and their sense that God's blessing rests upon his people not only when they gather in his house, but also when they go 'abroad' (i.e. out and about) on their daily occupations. Of this practice of processions through the fields Traherne says 'it sanctifieth the land in all our eyes'.

Here again he regrets that for fear of superstition this practice had been abandoned in some places. To him its advantages are manifest. 'There are some things that carry so much Light and Beauty with them that they need not be written in a Law, being asserted by Reason and Taught by Nature'.[14] So he argues that just as the worship of the temple in the Old Testament was beautified with music and dancing and processions, beyond anything prescribed in the law, so too the worship of the Church is adorned with outward ceremony and music, and particularly with this practice which links the blessing of God within the church building with the blessing of God abroad in all the world.

So the Church

> with an Incomparable Wideness and Depth of Wisdom hath added an Exterior Beauty, as well as an Interior within the Temple, that both without and within, in the fields and in the Churches, God being Honored, a Contemplating Ey might have the fuller Prospects, throughout all the Land, seeing the sitting of his Servants and the Majestie of his Service beneath the Roof, and the Goings of his Hosts abroad, in the open sun, Where by Ocular Demonstration, they might view His Works and see his Glory which they hear of in the Temple, and learn to have a Sacred esteem even of His very fields, becaus they are His who made the Heavens. That all the World might appear to be the House of God, by the Universality, Variety and Beauty of His Servants and their Ministery.[15]

So God's people learn to see in the world around them the glory which they hear of within his temple. By the universality, variety and beauty of their ministry they come to realise that the whole world is the house of God, filled with his glory. In the articulation of the Church's worship, in the celebration of the Church's year, in the maintenance of this partly ecclesiastical, partly popular custom of 'beating the bounds', something is revealed of the holiness of all things, the sacramental character of all creation. 'Your Enjoyment of the World is never right, till evry Morning you awake in Heaven: see yourself in your fathers Palace: and look upon the skies and the Earth and the Air as Celestial Joys ...' exclaims Traherne in a moment of heightened vision.[16] But that same vision was for him worked out in the very substance of his social living and his priestly ministry. It is perhaps one cause of his strength that he had been able to realise such a remarkable integration of inner and outer, private and public, secular and sacred, earthly and heavenly. Here in his writing about Rogation-tide, as in his poem 'Christmas Day' he manages to express in a striking way the unity of all things human and divine gathered together in the praise of the incarnate Word of God.[17]

I have tried to show in this essay how Traherne the poet, the man of a piercing and singular vision, is also Traherne the priest, the celebrant of the Church's liturgy, who offers up with all God's people, 'the sacrifice of praise and thanksgiving'. Thomas Merton in his tantalisingly brief comments on Traherne speaks of how when reading him 'we must penetrate immediately to the central intuition, a basic Eucharistic and primitive Christian theology of praise'. He goes on to quote some sentences from the 76th of the Second Century of Meditations. 'We infinitly wrong ourselves by Lazines and Confinement. All Creatures in all Nations and Tongues and Peoples Prais God infinitly; and the more for being your Sole and Perfect Treasures. You are never what you ought till you go out of yourself and walk among them.'[18] For Traherne this 'walking' among God's creatures was primarily a matter of thought and prayer, but it included actual, physical walking around the fields of his parish and the cities which he knew. This calling to praise which can unite us in ourselves and with one another in the human family, is a movement of appreciation and enjoyment which is surely vitally necessary to us if we are to learn how to cease from abusing and destroying the very fabric of the world in which God has placed us.

Thomas Traherne stands at a crucial moment in the development of the Anglican tradition, when the old world of the patristic and medieval synthesis was in touch with the first beginnings of the scientific movement represented by the Royal Society. He represents that tradition in seventeenth century Anglican thinking which turned to the Fathers, and especially the Greek Fathers, in its search for guidance through the hardening positions of reformation and counter-reformative controversy and at the same time remained eagerly open to new developments in human thought and research. The conclusions which the writers of that generation reached were in many ways tentative and incomplete. But they point us in a direction which is still of great significance, both in our ecumenical and in our ecological endeavours.

Notes

1. David Cecil, *Two Quiet Lives* (1948), pp. 6 - 7.
2. *Thomas Traherne* ed. H.M. Margoliouth (1958) Vol. I p. III.
3. Pre-eminently in the poem called 'The Retreat'. Henry Vaughan, *Poetry and Selected Prose*, ed. L.C. Martin (1963), p. 249.
4. Margoliouth. II. p. 326.
5. *The Papers of the Bibliographical Society of America*, Vol. 60 1966. 'Traherne's Church's Year Book', by Carol L. Marks, pp. 31 - 72.
6. *The Church's Year Book*, Bodleian ms. Eng. th.c.51. f. 46.
7. *Ibid*, ff. 48 - 9.
8. *Ibid*, ff. 100 - 101.
9. *The Works of George Herbert*, ed. F.E. Hutchinson (1953), 'To All Angels and Saints', pp. 77. - 78.
10. *op.cit*, p. 104.
11. The whole meditation, which was first published in an article in *Theology* in 1970, is to be found in A. M. Allchin, *The Joy of All Creation* (1984), pp. 86 - 87.
12. *op.cit*, ff. 22 - 3.
13. Hutchinson, pp. 283 - 4.
14. *op.cit*, f. 23.
15. *ibid*, f. 24.
16. Centuries I. 28.

17. For 'Christmas Day' and its implications for an understanding of Traherne see *The Joy of All Creation*, pp. 80 - 85.
18. Thomas Merton, *Mystics and Zen Masters* (1967), pp. 133 - 4.

I acknowledge with thanks the permission of Bodley's Librarian to make the quotations from the Bodleian ms. Eng. th. c.51.

Traherne from his Unpublished Manuscripts

JULIA J. SMITH

It was one of Thomas Traherne's characteristic beliefs that no event or human action could ever be lost, but that 'evry passage person & thing in all Ages' would be treasured up, 'the smallest Sand & sleightest Thought'. The remarkable story of the preservation and rediscovery of the Traherne manuscripts seems to vindicate Traherne's faith in the treasures so mysteriously stored up by the passing of time. These discoveries, for the most part made early in this century, have been recently augmented not only by the identification of *Select Meditations* in 1964, but by the announcement in 1982 of a new find, of a completely unknown and original work of Traherne's, which is physically the largest manuscript of all. This manuscript, entitled *Commentaries of Heaven*, had actually been rescued in about 1967 from a burning rubbish tip in South Lancashire. The book was slightly charred, but otherwise extremely well-preserved, and contained even the original pins with which Traherne had attached some added passages. Its authorship was not identified at the time and the owner later emigrated to Canada, taking the manuscript with him: not until fifteen years after its discovery, when it was shown to the History Department at Toronto University, was it recognized as being by Traherne.[1]

So we now have eight manuscripts of Traherne's writings, at least six of them largely in his own hand: a unique amount of manuscript material for any seventeenth-century English author. What I intend to do in this article is to make a few remarks about the manuscripts as a whole, and then to give a more detailed description of the two most recently discovered manuscripts, *Select Meditations* and *Commentaries*, which are not accessible to the general reader.

One of the most intriguing questions about all of the Traherne manuscripts is, where were they between Traherne's death in 1674 and their rediscovery? We now know something of their story during the nineteenth century, when various of the manuscripts were owned by a classical scholar, an Oxford student, a publisher, and a chaplain to the Archbishop of Canterbury. None of them knew who the author of their manuscripts was, although on the whole they took good care of them, and the value of the manuscripts in sale catalogues in fact declined during the nineteenth century.[2] Of what happened to the manuscripts after Traherne's death and during the eighteenth century, however, we know almost nothing.

Other puzzles are raised by the content of the manuscripts. Not all of them contain original works; three of them are simply notebooks for recording quotations from other writers. But the distinction between what is original and what is not is not always so clear; Traherne was a voracious maker of extracts, and he frequently blends them in, unacknowledged, with his own writing in such a way that they are now easily mistaken for his own work. Almost all of his original writings contain passages of this kind, the *Church's Year Book* a very large number, and there are without doubt sources for other passages which have not yet been recognized.

Identified extracts can, however, provide clues to another unresolved question, the dating of the manuscripts. Definite dates are very few, and apart from Philip Traherne's statement in the Early Notebook, 'Philip Traherne is the true owner of this booke Amen Anno Domini 1655', are mainly provided by quotations from published works. Rather more uncertain is the process of making deductions from the political and religious context in which the manuscripts seem to have been written; I will say more about this later. But of course we should like to be able to place them not only in relation to literary and political history, but also in relation to Traherne's own life. Here we have the additional problem that during the last few years, it has become increasingly clear that we know even less about Traherne's life than we thought we did, and that there is no documentary evidence for some of the events, and most of the dates, which have been offered to us by biographical accounts of him. We have little evidence, for example, for his supposed friendship with the devotional writer Mrs Susanna Hopton; we do not know when he was actually resident in Oxford, Credenhill, or London, and there is therefore very little basis for most of the attempts which have been made to associate any of Traherne's works with one of these places rather than another.

Another biographical puzzle is presented by the handwriting of the manuscripts. Although most of them are written in Traherne's own small, neat, and easily legible hand, almost all of them contain the handwriting of other people too. The only one of these hands which has been identified is that of his brother Philip, but there were at least two other people who were much more closely involved in the production of the manuscripts, either collaborating with Traherne in composition, or copying out large quantities of text at his direction. Writing was obviously not a solitary activity for Traherne. We have no idea of the identity of his assistants; clearly, if we knew it, it could provide important information about Traherne's friendships, and his whereabouts.

Select Meditations and *Commentaries* have their share of these uncertainties, but they each have too a very distinct character, contrasting with each other in style, purpose and subject matter, their intended audience, and their date. *Select Meditations* contains, like Traherne's *Centuries*, a series of short meditations arranged in groups of one hundred. Like the *Centuries* it is apparently unfinished, and as the first part of the manuscript is missing, the meditations extend from the eighty-second of the first century to the sixty-eighth of the fourth. It seems to be an earlier work than *Centuries*, so Traherne when he wrote the latter had used this structure before. Unlike most of the other Traherne manuscripts, *Select Meditations* is not the author's working copy; there are fairly clear indications that it is a fair copy made from an earlier draft, and the handwriting differs from that which we generally accept as Traherne's. Traherne probably did not make this copy of his work himself, but there are a few short passages apparently written in his characteristic hand, so that at least he seems to have been associated with the production of the manuscript.

The main evidence for dating the work is the allusions to public affairs which it contains. From its references to the king, it is clearly to be placed after the Restoration of Charles II in 1660: 'Soften our Kings Heart, Teach our Senators Wisdom' (I.82). But Traherne's pervasive anxiety in this work about the precarious nature of the settlement of church and state, and the dominance of his fears of protestant sectaries who oppose a national church, rather than of papists, seem to indicate that it was written not long after 1660. Indeed anxiety about the state of the nation, accompanied by intercession on its behalf, is one of the keynotes of *Select Meditations*. Traherne has persistently and mistakenly been thought of as a writer to whom political events and contexts are not of any significance. In fact he was very deeply involved in the events, issues and attitudes of his own time, and *Select Meditations* provides abundant evidence of this.

Like many religious writers of all persuasions, Traherne regarded the upheavals of seventeenth-century politics as a divine judgement on the sins of the nation, and in *Select Meditations* he reflected anxiously, 'The prophets and the preists are corrupted them selves from them prophaness is gon forth among the people. They know not me saith the Lord, they understand not my wayes nor the operation of my hands. Shall I not be Avenged of Such a Nation as this!' (I.85). Traherne's own thoughts of felicity are overshadowed by 'an Awfull Dread of his High Majestie & Great Judgments which have so latly happened' (II.42). 'Every way', he tells God, 'thou art provoked to Anger, by Open profaness and spirituall wickedness' (I.85), while Traherne sees his own role as

> to Lament the crimes
> Which here appear
> To wash the Times
> With Teares. (I.89)

But the sin which he most feared was a specifically political one: opposition to the unity of the national church. In one meditation, he rhetorically addresses nonconformists: 'Do you verily beleiv it unlawfull for Kings & parliaments & Elders in a National Manner to Covenant with God' (III.25). He attacks 'Ignorant Zealots' who reject the concept of a national church, and he offers his own vision of it: 'when they Move by Consent like an united Army: How Ravishing is their Beauty, How sweet their Order! It is O my God as if the Nation had but one Soul' (I.85). At the same time, he admits the falsity of kings and magistrates who 'have offer'd up their Scepters at the feet of

Christ. That they are not Sincere in their Interior man is their Eternal Shame' (III.23). *Select Meditations*, in fact, like all of Traherne's writing, is much preoccupied with ideas and imagery of kingship, which in view of the political context in which Traherne was writing, when in his lifetime one king had been executed and another restored, cannot be seen entirely in spiritual terms. Complementary meditations reflect on the nature of temporal and spiritual power. Traherne offers an ideal of kingship:

> O How Divine & Greatly Blessed is the Life of Holy Kings! which excelleth here in Temporal Things & forever resteth among the Holy Angels. is nourished here with Earthly Delights is clothed there with Eternal Glory ... here weareth a Regal crown there Danceth with Eternal Joy. (II.81)

But at the same time he maintains, in a way which would have seemed subversive to his contemporaries, that everyone else could be a king too: 'If I live truely in the Divine Image I shall appear among Kings a Greater King' (III.15). In a discussion of the source of the earthly king's power, he exclaims, 'Lord what is a Thousand Kingdoms, compared to mans Dominion over the world. Can hats & Knees & Thrones & scepters & silver & Gold & splendid Palaces, appear any other then Shells and patches and Tincell vanities, when they are put in Competition with all the Gloryes of Heaven & Earth!' (III.10).

In parallel with these public concerns, made perhaps more explicit in *Select Meditations* than in many of Traherne's other writings, are very personal meditations, in which Traherne no less voices anxiety about himself and his own calling. One of the links between them is the fact that Traherne casts himself as an intercessor on behalf of the nation: 'I beseech Thee to hear my Daylie prayers. Save this Nation, spare thy people' (I.82); and that the extent of the wickedness which he perceives makes him doubt his own persistence in prayer: 'O my God I could be Quickly weary Quickly weary both of Repenting and Interceding. But thy Lov is the encourager of mine' (I.84). He reflects on his own ministry, the sense of responsibility derived from his educational advantages: 'I who have been nourished at universities in Beautifull Streets & famous Colledges, & am sent thither from God Almighty the maker of Heaven & Earth, to teach Immortal Souls the way to Heaven' (III.83). 'God hath use now', he reflects, 'for an Holy man, which maketh Him more precious than the Golden wedge of Ophir, use for him Greater than what Angels are Admitted to more Sublime then any Employment that Adam had in Eden, namely the calling of those wonderfull ones to their Ancient possessions, to the Enjoyment of God, to their Inheritance of the world, to the Recovery of their Blessedness' (II.15). *Select Meditations* both celebrates those eternal joys, the opportunity we are given of living the best of all possible lives, when we realize that holiness and happiness are one, and also laments the difficulty of teaching this to others: 'And when I enter into Houses let me remember the Glory I saw in the feilds and the Blessedness of thy Kingdom! it is imposible at once to be present with men & Thee my God, unless we oppose and Greive at their Thoughts ... their thoughts will lead us out of thy presence' (II.100). There are passages of spiritual autobiography, such as are familiar from the *Centuries*: 'In my Close Retirements I was some years as if no Body but I had been in the world. ... And I had nothing to do but walk with God, as if there had been non other but He and I' (III.69). In another passage he recalls, 'This Endless Comprehension of my Immortal Soul when I first saw it, so wholy Ravished and Transported my spirit, that for a fortnight after I could scarsly Think or speak or write of any other Thing. But Like a man Doteing with Delight and Extasie, Talk of it Night and Day as if all the Joy of Heaven & Earth were Shut up in it. For in very Deed there I saw the Divine Image Relucent & Shining' (IV.3). There are also detailed instructions on how to live the life of blessedness, 'Instructions so Great, that I would have given in my childhood Millions of worlds to have met with one teaching them' (III.31).

There is no indication of the purpose for which Traherne wrote *Select Meditations*, or for what audience such 'Instructions Teaching us how to Liv the Life of Happieness' (III.31) were intended, although the fact that the manuscript is a fair copy does suggest that we cannot view them simply as a private and spontaneous expression of feeling. In contrast with this, the purpose and scope of the most recently discovered manuscript, *Commentaries of Heaven*, is fully described by Traherne on the elaborate title-page which begins the manuscript:

COMMENTARIES
of Heaven.
WHEREIN
The Mysteries of Felicitie
are opened:
and
ALL THINGS
Discovered
to be
Objects of Happiness.
EVRY BEING
Created & Increated
being Alphabeticaly Represented
As it will appear
In the Light
of
GLORY
Wherein also
For the Satisfaction of Atheists, & the Consolation
of Christians, as well as the Assistance & Encouragement
of Divines: the Transcendent Verities
of the Holy Scriptures, & the
Highest Objects of the Christian faith are
in a Clear Mirror Exhibited to the
Ey of Reason: in their Realitie and
Glory.

Traherne had criticized his Oxford education because 'There was never a Tutor that did professely Teach Felicity' (*Centuries*, III.37). *Commentaries of Heaven* is a deliberate corrective to this deficiency because its aim, in every subject it discusses, is to show how all human knowledge pertains to the 'Certain End' of felicity. It does not confine itself to branches of learning which are obviously theological or religious, but tackles some of those same subjects, such as astronomy, arithmetic, and Aristotle's philosophy, which Traherne had felt to be imperfectly taught at Oxford. His book is to complement that education; as he explains carefully in his discussion of 'Arithmetick':

Numeration, Addition Division, Multiplication, Subtraction ... &c. are its parts. With which if you desire further to be acquainted consult with the Books of Arithmetick that are already extant. For our Designe is only to supply the Defects of Learning as much as possible; and to refer the Readers for common Subjects already treated on to the Books that pass up and down vulgarly about them. unless in some peculiar Cases of Extraordinary use & importance, for the immediate Instruction of Man in felicity. (f. 130v.1)

This survey of the whole of human knowledge was a very ambitious project. Traherne did not live to complete it, and it is hard to see how it could have been completed on the scale on which it was begun. As the title-page suggests, every subject is 'Alphabeticaly Represented'; that is, the work is an alphabetical encyclopedia. In fact, Traherne got only as far as the beginning of the letter B, but the range of topics which he considered, from 'Abhorrence' to 'Bastard', accounts for ninety completed articles, eighty-two under the letter A and eight under B. The scale of the work is massive. The manuscript itself is a large one, measuring about twelve and a half by eight inches, and it contains nearly four hundred pages of small writing in double columns. It has been calculated that it is about 350,000 words long – as much again as all the writings of Traherne which have hitherto been published.

I think we have to assume that it was Traherne's premature death which prevented him from continuing it, because there is no sign that he himself was becoming discouraged by the thought of its ultimate unwieldiness. He probably would not have thought it unwieldy however long or repetitive it became. As he had complained in *Select Meditations* about other people's response to his message: 'Redundanc is Apprehended even in those Things of which there can be never Enough' (III.65). 'We have millions of Things to utter and Declare ... But must utter them by Drops; becaus they seem Dull and Dubious. O the misery of confined Man!' (III.66). Many of the headings for the rest of the alphabet were already worked out, and finished articles frequently give cross references to them, ranging from Bounty to Zeal. For example, Traherne urges the reader under 'Baseness', 'vid. Redemption. Incarnation. Passion. Christ. &c.'.

That it was Traherne's death which cut short his work on *Commentaries* also seems likely because we know that he was working on it in the 1670s, and therefore near the end of his life. Referring to the subject of Roman forgeries, he comments, 'Concerning which we shall say nothing here, bec. we have prepared a whole Tract upon that Theme (an intire volume) fit to be published' (f. 104v.2). We know that Traherne was preparing his *Roman Forgeries* for publication during 1673, and it was actually entered in the Stationers' Register on 25 September of that year. *Commentaries* also contains a number of quotations from a book published in 1670 – Theophilus Gale's *Court of the Gentiles*. The quotations from Gale also link *Commentaries* with Traherne's Commonplace Book. This notebook is bound in with the poems which were identified by Dobell, and it consists of a series of extracts from Gale and other writers copied out under alphabetical headings, from 'Aristotles Philosophie' to 'Virtue'. Its purpose, ever since its discovery, has been something of a mystery, but we can now see that it was compiled with the preparation of *Commentaries* in mind. Most of the Commonplace Book's entries under A reappear in *Commentaries*: 'Aristotles Philosophie', 'Of Judicial Astrologie', 'Atoms', and 'Authoritie', as well as a large number of common headings for which Traherne did not complete the entries.

Unlike some of the other manuscripts, the purpose of which remains unclear, there is no doubt that *Commentaries of Heaven* was intended by Traherne for publication. We can see this from the existence of the title-page, from the prospective readers described on it, and from the work's air of addressing a large audience – even though, like the other manuscripts, it is not signed. Traherne exhorts the 'Beloved Reader'; leaves a difficult question unresolved to exercise 'the Soul of the Reader' (f. 4v.2); and suggests further reading. He also gives more detailed directions to those readers, such as the 'refined Atheist' who may be in need of advice: 'He is troubled that God is Invisible, & prone to believ that there are no Invisible Things at all: But if he will look for the word, *Invisible*: he shall be satisfied' (f. 163v.2). Or when discussing a difficult subject, he warns: 'I would hav the Reader to beware ... this Discours is Dedicated only to Publick Persons, that are the Watchmen & Bulwarks of Christianity' (f. 17r.2).

The articles themselves cover an enormous variety of topics, including subjects which are obviously related to felicity, such as 'Abundance', 'Adoration', 'Almighty', and 'Angell'; and those which are not, like 'Adulterie', 'Anger', 'Apostasie', and 'Arithmetick'. Part of the attraction of the work is the fascination of seeing how Traherne is able to make unlikely subjects appear in the light of felicity; as he remarks in his discussion of 'Anger', 'The true End of so unprofitable a passion it is difficult to find. It is so clouded with the Abuse of it, that the Good is unknown' (f. 98r.1). But Traherne, of course, is able to find it. Equally ingenious is the way in which he links apparently disparate subjects together; moving on from 'Babe' to 'Babel', for example, he remarks, 'When we enter first upon the years of Discretion, we find ourselves Babes still to the forrein Nations and Kingdoms on Earth: for by reason of the variety of Languages, we are dumb (as it were) to all men but those of our own Country' (f. 191v.1).

The articles vary enormously in length, from 'Balme' occupying just over one column of the manuscript, to 'Ages' occupying thirty-eight. Typically the articles are divided into numerous short sections, with their own headings. For example, under 'Backsliding' we find 'Its Signification', 'Its Original', 'Its Deformitie & Guilt', 'A Backsliders Hope', 'His Duty', and a short poem. Often articles end with a collection of aphorisms, and scriptural references. *Commentaries* is mainly written in prose; although many of the articles end with verses, their poetic quality is not high. Traherne uses them simply to reinforce points which he had already made in the prose. In one article, Traherne makes a note to himself, 'Consider Whether it be not best leav out some of these Poems' (f. 172r.2).

It is in the prose that we find writing equal to Traherne's best, both on themes of the kind which are already valued and expected in him, and on less expected subjects. All of Traherne's characteristic themes appear, often developed in much greater detail than elsewhere in his writing: the themes of the infinity of space and the limitless capacity of the soul, the abundance of treasures, our potential for living in the image of God, the necessity of free will, the joys of Adam in Eden, and the much greater joys of the redeemed. For example, in a long article entitled 'Adam', Traherne describes Adam's response to the world when he 'first awaked out of his Dust':

On a suddain therfore being surprized with so much Beauty, Wideness, State & Splendor he was Ravished, & all at once seeing from whence, & by whom, & to what he was raised, his first Thought was a Mixture of Reverence Admiration Gratitude & Joy attending the World he conceived in his Mind. (f. 37v.2–38r.1)

Another characteristic theme is illustrated by his description of the capacity of the soul under the heading 'All Things':

I found the Desires of the Soul to be Insatiable and its powers Endless; & Knew by nature that they were not made in vain. ... I saw I could prize things beyond the Heavens, pierce into the Centre, expatiat over all Ages, be present in Paradice, & at our Saviors Cross. (f. 78v.1)

'Admiration' too is a heading we might have expected: 'as evry Power is a New Room in the Soul, wherin Treasures of another Kind might be reposited; so is this a Treasurie for Wonders. ... Wonderfulness it self would be in vain, were there no Power prepard to Wonder' (f. 41r.1). Less obvious is Traherne's admiration under 'Account' at bills of mortality and 'Poll-Bils for Taxes' (f. 22v.1); accounting is, he reflects, 'from Merchants Shops & Princes Courts taken up into Heaven; and shineth there like a star in GODS Kingdom' (f. 22r.2).

Many of the articles provide further evidence of Traherne's interest in contemporary events and intellectual developments. He continues to reflect on political affairs, condemning the Restoration court in his only known attempt at a satirical poem, in the words:

Princes are bruitish & nobles are beasts,
While panders & Queans are their Guests. (f. 47v.2)

The article 'Authority' contains further discussion of the theory of kingship: 'When I consider the Authority that Kings & Princes hav over the persons Liberties Lives & Estates of their Subjects, & see a single person reigning so absolutely over innumerable thousands, all by Nature equal to himself, & many by Grace & Wisdom above him, Authority seemeth the Greatest Wonder in the World' (f. 187r.1). There is also a great deal of reference to contemporary theological controversy: in addition to extended attacks on the Roman Catholic church under the headings 'Antichrist' and 'Antiquity', reflecting the national anti-Catholic ferment of the early 1670s, there is also criticism of various groups of protestant nonconformists. Traherne attacks Baptists, Socinians and Quakers, the last being 'more corrupt in his Intellectuals than they all; his portion (certainly without Repentance) is in the Lake that burneth with fire & Brimstone' (f. 137r.1). In the preface to *Roman Forgeries*, Traherne printed a spirited account of his skirmish with a Roman Catholic opponent. He obviously liked the picture of himself as a ready controversialist, and *Commentaries* gives us several fascinating glimpses into this aspect of his character. Under 'Baptism', he recounts his two meetings with John Tombes, the 'great Ringleader' of the Anabaptists, who held public debates on the subject of infant baptism. Twice he put the same question to Tombes, and, according to Traherne, 'he was both times as Blank, & mute as a Fish' (f. 194r.2-v.1). Traherne adds that he had 'reason to believ he was condemned of his Conscience'. Under 'Ascension', he gives another example of his controversial prowess: 'it is the Easiest thing in the World to convince & confound a Jew, as I my self have done, out of the Books of the O. Test.' (f. 139v.1). This is particularly interesting since Jews had only recently been readmitted to England.

Commentaries, however, contains little biographical information about Traherne. Accounts of his spiritual development, of a familiar kind, do occasionally appear: 'From mine Infancy indeed I did long after Happiness, and thought it must be infinit. But little did I think it was so infinit. I thirsted & Desired & Coveted Enjoyments, but they were unknown: & abov the Stars, among the Holy Angels thought I, but denied to Men in this World! I questioned whether it was possible there should be a GOD, & I so Poor? and Men so Miserable?' (f. 11v.2). But personal passages of this kind are infrequent, and references to the external events of Traherne's life even more so. There are a few other intriguing biographical allusions which also reflect Traherne's interest in natural history. In his discussion of 'Appetite', he describes how he has 'seen an Ape sit in a chimnie Corner' which 'with the fingers of a man … seemed to pick off the litle filmes & loose fragments of the fish that were broyling on the Coals' (f. 114v.1-2). And in discussing 'Ant', he describes at length some experiments carried out by a friend, 'a Knight, and a Traveller, that hath made som curious Observations' on this insect (f. 101r.1).

Commentaries provides ample evidence of Traherne's interest in many aspects of contemporary science, including articles under the headings 'Air', 'Ant', 'Arithmetick', 'Astronomie', 'Astrologie', and 'Atom', which combine descriptions of experiments and speculation about recent discoveries with some fine descriptive writing. Under 'Atom', Traherne offers his opinions 'for the Compleating of the Body of Natural Philosophie', and ponders at great length and with great enthusiasm on the atom's paradoxical nature: 'An Atom is a marvellous Effect of Almighty Power, or a great Miracle in a litle Room: perhaps I may say, it is an infinit Miracle in no Room. for it is so small, that it taketh up no place at all, but filleth an indivisible point of Space only' (f. 164v.1). He is attracted by the infinitely small and the infinitely large. Under 'Astronomie', he is uncertain whether or not to accept new astronomical theories, and wonders whether it is the earth which moves or the stars, but concludes: 'Whether they stand still, or move, som what moves, & the Swiftness is Incredible. As the Wisdom is, wherby they are made to move so silently, that all things seem to be quiet, in so vast an Hurry; & so mysteriously, that whether they move or noe ... we cannot tell, all things are so full of Wonder, & Secret Depth to Mans Understanding' (f. 161r.1). His receptiveness to new ideas was moulded by his theological aims; whatever the astronomical facts, they would evoke admiration from him at God's best-of-all-possible worlds.

This quotation from 'Astronomie' makes it clear too that science, like everything else, was not of importance for Traherne in itself, but only, to come back to the title-page of *Commentaries*, as it could be represented 'In the Light of GLORY'. And this was true of everything which he wrote. It has been very rightly remarked by Allan Pritchard that 'Despite the apparent variety of subjects Traherne has ultimately only one subject',[3] and this is the case not only of *Commentaries* but of all his other writings, which could be seen as part of its all-embracing theme. Art itself, as *Commentaries* tells us, was of value to Traherne only in so far as it was joined with virtue in the artist: 'But a Wise Man feeds upon all Arts & turnes them into Nourishment ... Admiring the

Excellency of Humane Nature, but his more, which hath given such Power unto Men' (f. 134r.1). Conversely, however, in the light of felicity, all subjects and objects were his to possess through love and understanding. All Things, Traherne reflected under that heading, are ours; but they 'serv us most in being made conformable to our Fathers pleasure, in manifesting forth his Glory' (f. 79r.1). And we too are to remember in studying Traherne that, as he wrote in 'Admiration', 'all the End of our Learning & Study is that we may be able to Wonder at GOD' (f. 42r.2).

Notes

Quotations from *Select Meditations* are taken from the unpublished manuscript in the Beinecke Library at Yale University. I would like to thank Professor Louis Martz for supplying me with a microfilm of this manuscript, and the Curator of the Osborn Collection for permission to quote from it.

Quotations from *Commentaries of Heaven* are taken from the unpublished manuscript in the British Library.

In all quotations from these manuscripts, Traherne's original spelling, punctuation and capitalization have been preserved, but standard abbreviations have been expanded.

1. The discovery of *Commentaries* is announced in Elliott Rose, 'A New Traherne Manuscript', *TLS*, 19 March 1982, p. 324.
2. For an account of some of these owners, see Hilton Kelliher, 'The Rediscovery of Thomas Traherne', *TLS*, 14 September 1984, p. 1038.
3. Allan Pritchard, 'Traherne's *Commentaries of Heaven*', *University of Toronto Quarterly*, 53 (1983), 1-35.

Appendix

Select Meditations

II.66

Those that think our union with God so Incredible. are taught more in the Sacrament. He gives Himselfe to be our food. is united to us. Incorporated in us, for what doth he intimate by the Bread & wine, but as the Bread & wine are Mingled with our flesh, and is nourishment Diffused through all our members. So he is Lov mingling with our Lov as flame with flame, knowledge shining in our knowledge as Light with Light. An omnipresent Sphere within our Sphere.

II.77

Love is the onely sacrifice. It is Like our Saviour its own Preist and its own Alter. Perfume and flame. A Prophet Preist and King. O my God it is like thy Son, the Phænix of the world. Its comprehensiv sphere, a flaming Temple. The Antitipe of her who is the faigned Miracle of all the Birds and more then so. Its own Alter fire nest and Sacrifice. O Thou Nest, and Bed of Spices! In its Highest Agonies. ever Dying, Expiring and Reviving every moment.

III.30

When I come from the Scholes, haveing there heard them dispute De Ente, De forma materiali, D[e] Quid-ditate; and such like Drie and Empty Theames: when I came from the Heathen Poets, Having seen their vanities Dreames & fables. or else from the market haveing there seen a great deal of chaffering about cloth and Money, & things more Drie than Hæcceitas & fables. yea when I come from Taverns haveing there seen Roaring Boys. that can swear & swagger & wallow in their vomitt: O what a Glorious thing is that Kingdom which in the Temple I behold! How doth it overflow with Living waters to Refresh a Droughty Soul. whence ever I come I find it. Amiable and Sweet. my only & resting Place. Seas of Amber or far more Rich, Mountains of Gold, or far Better, Territories more Kingly, then Angels else can tell How to frame. Laws Sweeter than the Hony Comb, souls & mansions more wide then the Heavens, such Heavens as Adam saw, affections Better then Sun Beams, yet Sun Beams Better than Rivers of Melted

Pearl, Golden Thrones & crowns of Love, and all these endlessly multiplied in all Ages. O the joy the food the satisfaction! where ever else I am, being a Stranger unto these I am a Husk with Swine. Not a Prodigal but a very Husk among them. A Husk in respect of Emptines. A Prodigal in respect of want, Nor ever am I Happy till I return Home.

III.83

When I see a Little Church Environed with Trees. how many Things are there which mine Eye discerneth not. The Labor of them which in Ancient Ages Builded it; the conversion of a Kingdom to God from Paganism, its protection by Laws, its subjection to Kings, its Relation to Bishops, usefulness & convenience for the Entertainment of Christians The Divine Service, office of the ministery, Solemn Assemblies Prayses & Thanksgivings, for the sake of which it was permitted, is Governed, standeth & flourisheth. Perhaps when I Look upon it, it is Desolate & Empty almost Like an heap of Stones: non of these things appearing to the Eye, which nevertheless are the Spirituall Beauties which adorn & clothe it. The uses Relations services & Ends being the Spiritual & Invisible Things: that make any material to be of worth. He that cannot see Invisible cannot Enjoy nor valu Temples. But He that seeth them may Esteem them all to be his own: & wonder at the Divine Bounty for giving them so Richly becaus were there non such, & he able to Erect them, for these End[s] it were very Amiable that Himselfe should Endow them. The Services are such that He should Delight in; & becaus so rejoyce in God for preparing them to his Hands. Especialy I who have been nourished at universities in Beautifull Streets & famous Colledges, & am sent thither from God Almighty the maker of Heaven & Earth, to teach Immortal Souls the way to Heaven, to sanctifie his Sabbaths, to instruct them in his Laws Given upon mount Sinay, & to shew them the Lov of a Glorious Saviour Slain upon mount Calvary: to Lead them by his Merrits to Eternal Joys.

Commentaries of Heaven, Ages

The Delights of Ages Their Commonness

When I devoted my self to Study, and spend my Days as consecrated to felicitie, I neither knew its Objects nor the maner of enjoying them. being therfore Stark Blind, notwithstanding those Rays and Shreds of

Learning I had gathered, Learning was like a Wide & infinit Ocean; I saw no Haven nor End to which I might Stear, and therfore no Objects, because all, innumerable, and Endless. For which cause fearing least I should miss in my Choise of Objects, and wast all my Time in vain I prayed that GOD would direct me to the Best. And beginning to consider which they were I rememberd, that GODS Goodness was infinit, and so was his Bounty & Love in like maner. And that therfore in all likelyhood the Best things were not they that are most Scarce but most Common. For where Goodness is infinit, nothing can make a Thing scarce but the vileness of it. Then I examined the matter by enquiring more deeply into the Nature of things: & found, that Gold Silver & Jewels were Scarce: but Fruits & Flowers Common, Bread Earth Air Water Light, the Skie, the Sun & Stars, Men Beasts Fowles & fishes the Laws of GOD and Angels the Holy Scriptures, our Saviors Cross, the Glad Tidings of the Gospel &c. I could scarce invent a true & real use of the scarce things But the necessity & serviceableness of the other was infinite, or els their pleasure Dignity and Excellency, which commended their valu to me. Then I called to mind the Blindness and Corruption of men: how having Eys they see not, ears & hear not hearts and understand not. & that perhaps they were as Cross and pervers in their Opinions and Choises as in their Corruptions: Yea that an Error here may be one of the greatest. And I realy found that Common Things at last were most Excellent & therfore resolvd to study the Laws & Ways & Works of GOD, which were so Common that they filled all Ages and all worlds and were to my Hopes most Excellent becaus most Common. Thus was I guided to the most Excellent Things purely by the Indication of their Commonness. And since I have found Man to be a Centre in Worlds of felicitie, and my self a Sphere of infinit Centres. And that their Commonness and presence ought not to destroy the Angels Joys.

Commentaries of Heaven, Ancestor

That our Interest lies much in former Ages, we see by our Ancestors, who live to us as yet in those invisible & mysterious Rooms, which tho they seemed transeunt in passing by, are now fixt & permanent forever.

That our Ancestors themselvs are Objective Joys, is evident, because 1. They are the Root of our Being, 2. We are the Branches of theirs. 3. They are the fountains of many Benefits, 4. We are the objects of their Lov, 5. And they of ours. 6. They are Blessed in their

Seed, And we in our forefathers. Nature has given us a power to enter Spiritualy in unto them, & the Rayes of their understanding can Extend unto us. We are in our Ancestors united, they are in us multiplied. We are made to Enjoy communion with each other. In the Direct Line we are all the first Degree of Kindred to 1000. generations. If we lov them as ourselvs, we are as Happy in them as in our selvs. They love us, I think more than themselvs. For children are their fathers Bowels, & the Apple of their Ey: yet Grandfathers lov their Grand-children, more than fathers their children, liv in them & feel in them, as we see by their fondness: so that the further off we go, the more naturaly their Lov doth increas, & the more they delight in our Blessedness. Tis our Duty to think on these things, to see the Beauty of Truth, to prize the Blessings in all Ages of which we are partakers, & to prais God for them. We ought not to coop up our understandings, or to imprison our Souls in Cubs, which were made to expatiate over all the World, to liv in Communion, & to walk with GOD as Enoch did in all Ages.

They multiply our fruitions. One would think the Sun could do me no Service but in mine own Age; & that the moon & stars could not attend upon me but within the confines of mine own Life, & that the Duration of my Existence was the Measure of their continuance & Ministery to me, the Termes or Limits of my Life, my Birth & Death bounding all my fruitions & Enjoyments of them. But all the Creatures in Heaven & Earth appear in Ages & so many true & real Worlds salute mine Ey as there are Generations. Som one or other of my Ancestors lived in them all. The Sun gave him Light, the Moon Refreshment, the Earth nourishment, the Sea moysture, the Air Breath, & fire Warmth, & all these assisted him, that he might live & beget me. The Influences of all the Stars, & of all other things in that Age descend upon me, extend to me, & rest in me; & that perhaps 10000. Ways exciting my Praises.

The Omnipresence of GOD, or his Almighty power exprest in one Effect is not sufficient for me, it is again enjoyed in evry person among all my Ancestors, & so is his Goodness Lovingkindness & Glory, in their Exaltation & Blessedness.

I lov my Ancestors, becaus they gave me my Being; & I owe all that I am or have unto them: They are in some respect the fountain of all my Joy & Glory: Evry one is wholy: for my Hope had been Extinct, had any of them perisht before I had been conceived: Tho they all are but one Chanell of my conveyance from Adam. The Maner of our Generation is a Curious piece, & full of Mysteries.

My Ancestors were all made in the Divine Image, & redeemed by the Blood of Christ as well as I; & they are all as well as I Heirs of Eternal Glory. They prais God, with the Glorious Company of the Apostles prais him, with the Goodly fellowship of the Prophets prais him, with the Noble Army of Martyrs prais him: with all his Hosts admire him, minister before his Throne, & assist us to lov & adore him: Who being Wise & Holy delight in these services beyond Measure.

GOD Angels & Men loved them, & they are before the face of GOD forever. In GOD we lov them Eternaly. We lov them for the Angels sake, for the Angels lov them, & take pleasure to see the Object of their Lov beloved, & in them we admire the Holy Angels.

As Abel by his faith yet speaketh, so do they by their Example, Life Profession Death & victory. They live unto us still & the seeds of their Lov in secret laid up are most real Treasures.

There is not a Morsel of Bread which they did ever eat, but it served us in feeding them & the Sun & Moon & Stars, the four Elements Earth Water Air Light & fire, the powers & Influences of all the World, served us in preparing the Corn that made that Bread. We are able to rejoyce in it, & it is our Duty.

All the Goodness of GOD to them is Goodness to us. His infinit Wisdom hath infinitly magnified his Almighty Power, by multiplying to us the Fruition of his Goodness for the increase of Infinit Blessedness, for his far more than infinit & Eternal Glory.

John Baptist was Precursor to our Lord
The Ages in my Ancestors afford
Me many Predecessors, that prepard
The way, as if my God did still regard
In making them my Soul alone, who am
The very End, the End for which they came
Into the World. For they are evry one
My father still, & I his Son alone.
If they begot me any more, that other
Is a new Gift: for he is still my Brother.